Transforming Your Self-Image

Vikki Burke

Unless otherwise indicated, all Scripture quotations are taken from the *New American Standard Version*.

The Amplified Bible © The Lockman Foundation, La Habra, California, 1954, 1958.

New Living Translation © 1996. Tyndale House Publishers, Inc., Wheaton, Illinois.

The Holy Bible, New King James Version © 1982. Thomas Nelson, Inc., Nashville, Tennessee.

The New Testament in Modern English by J. B. Phillips © 1961, The MacMillian Company, New York, New York.

New American Standard Bible © 1960, 1962, 1963, 1968, 1971, 1972, 1973, 1975, 1994 by the Lockman Foundation.

The Holy Bible, New International Version © 1973, 1978, 1994 by the International Bible Society. Zonervan Publishing House.

Transforming Your Self-Image

ISBN 978-1-890026-11-0
© 2001 by Vikki Burke

Dennis Burke Ministries
P. O. Box 150043
Arlington, TX 76015

CONTENTS

Learn to Master Your Thoughts………5

Distorted Mirrors and Images………15

Strongholds of the Mind…………..23

Transforming Distorted Images………35

Meditation is the Key…...…………41

Proof of Love……………………...51

Chapter 1 ─────────────

Learn to Master
Your Thoughts

D o you want to boost your faith in God's ability to bring His will to pass in your life? Then stop agreeing with what others say about you and learn to master your thoughts.

Far too often we underestimate God's ability to bring His will to pass in our lives. And one of the main reasons is because we have believed what others have said about us instead of what God has said.

What difference does it make? Proverbs 23:7 makes the importance of our thought lives completely clear: "For as a man thinks within himself, so he is."

Impossible thinking can only produce impossible living. In the same way, small thinking will cause you to live far below the standard God desires for you—He is a big God! When you feel limited in what you can do, your thinking will confine you to those boundaries, but God is limitless. He wants to raise you to a new level of thinking which will raise you to a higher degree of living!

The daily challenge you and I face is to train ourselves to think from God's perspective—not man's. God sees us in the light of the finished work of Jesus, not based on our achievement or outward appearance. Notice the strong words Jesus spoke to Peter concerning viewing things from man's point of view:

6

"Out of My way, Satan! You stand right in my path, Peter, when you look at things from man's point of view and not God's" (Matthew 16:23 *J.B. Phillips*).

Do you realize that you can actually stand in God's way when you look at things from your own, limited perspective? You certainly don't want to be responsible for hindering God's plan, do you? No, you want to cooperate with Him in every way possible.

The Lord demonstrated His point of view to the prophet Samuel while choosing a king for Israel:

"The Lord does not look at the things man looks at. Man looks at the outward appearance, but the

7

Lord looks at the heart" (1 Samuel 16:7 *NIV*).

This Scripture contrasts the way in which God looks at a person and the way humans judge. When Israel chose a king that pleased the people he was handsome in appearance. But when God chose a king, He chose a man after God's heart.

You see what a person looks like externally—you see their nose, eyes, hair, weight and judge accordingly. But Jesus exposed human nature when He said, "You judge according to the flesh" (John 8:15). Instead, God sees you for who you really are because He sees the thoughts and intents of the heart.

According to Hebrews 4:12 your thoughts and the motivation of your heart interact significantly:

"For the word of God is living and active and sharper than any two-edged sword, and piercing as far as the division of soul and spirit, of both joints and marrow, and able to judge the thoughts and intentions of the heart."

You are mistaken if you assume the law of sowing and reaping doesn't apply to the things you dwell on. The Word of God discerns not only your deeds, but the thoughts and intentions of your heart as well. If you know God is observing your thoughts, you ought to scrutinize them yourself.

The reason a close scrutiny of your thought life is so important is that you cannot separate what you think from how you live. Right thinking will always produce righteous living.

Notice what Proverbs 12:5 says about your thoughts, "A good man's mind is filled with honest thoughts" (*AMP*).

Proverbs 15:26 says in contrast: "The thoughts of the wicked are shamefully vile and exceedingly offensive to the Lord" (*AMP*).

Which of these two verses more accurately depicts your thought life? Can the Lord rely on your thoughts? Are they honest or are they shameful and offensive to Him? Let me ask you the same question He asked me: "Do your thoughts glorify God, or horrify God?"

Do You Have a Grasshopper Mentality?

The Scripture makes it clear that your thoughts are directly correlated in shaping your actions. In fact, your thoughts and imaginations will eventually direct your actions—whether godly or ungodly.

When Moses sent twelve men into the land of Cana as spies, ten returned reporting, "We became like grasshoppers in our own sight, and so we were in their sight" (Numbers 13:33).

In reality, the spies couldn't possibly have known how their enemy viewed them without asking them. And we know any conversation with the residents of Jericho would have exposed their identity and resulted in execution.

However, their report does shine light on how they viewed themselves—as insignificant and inadequate. They saw themselves as nothing more than insects to be crushed under their enemies' foot. But God did not see them that way.

Not only were the spies limited by their thinking, but they infected everyone who believed their report with the same hopeless attitude. It didn't take long before everyone except two men believed that Israel was incapable of possessing what God had already promised them. As a result, every person who believed the distorted report of the ten spies died in the wilderness except Joshua and Caleb.

It was Israel's thinking—not the will of God—that determined their destiny. They were literally robbed of the promise of God because they chose to believe the wrong report.

You and I are waging a war over who will govern our thoughts, and whoever controls our thoughts controls our destiny. The choices we make will determine the outcome!

Do you realize that just because something is the will of God it doesn't mean that it will automatically come to pass? We know according to John 3:16 that it is not God's will that any should perish, but people die and go to hell everyday because they will not make the decision to turn their lives over to Jesus.

What made the difference between the ten spies and Joshua and Caleb? All twelve spies saw the same giants, but instead of focusing on the giants, Joshua and Caleb kept their eyes on the promise of God.

When you refuse to believe anything that contradicts God's Word—regardless of the giants you face—then whatever God has promised you will come to pass in your life just like it did in Joshua and Caleb's. However, if you don't purposely

13

take charge of your thoughts, you will be influenced by the negative reports of the world just like the children of Israel were influenced by the negative report of the ten spies.

Chapter 2

Distorted Mirrors and Images

Have you ever been to an amusement park that had those funny shaped mirrors? There are mirrors that make you look really tall and thin. Others that make you look short and wide. There is also a mirror that makes you wide in the middle while your legs and neck look skinny.

Words spoken by significant people in your life—friends, a spouse, parents, teachers or an employer—can affect you like the amusement park mirrors. When you allow the opinions of others to determine your perspective, the image you have about yourself can become distorted in the same way the amusement park mirrors distort your body—and the more warped the mirror the more distorted the image.

You may have a difficult time seeing yourself the way God sees you because the mirrors that have reflected your image have been distorted. If you have looked into a distorted mirror all of your life you will believe the distorted image the mirror reflects.

The reason you are able to laugh at the distorted mirrors at an amusement park is because you have accurate mirrors at home that reveal your true image.

The world's answer to this sense of inadequacy is to develop a healthy self-image. But their concept of a self-image differs greatly from God's original intention for mankind. Any time you measure yourself by the world's standard you will fall short of God's glorious plan.

God's Original Plan

According to Genesis 1:26 God created you in His image and likeness. You must begin to see yourself that way. To merely build what the world terms a healthy self-image is to fall short of God's divine purpose and could possibly cause you to miss your God-given destiny.

If the world is influencing and molding your thoughts you will become just as confused as they are. For example, in the '80's the world promoted the concept of "I'm OK, You're OK." Then, in the '90's they decided I'm dysfunctional and you're dysfunctional. Are you as curious as I am about what they will promote in the decades to come?

Romans 12:2 from the *J.B. Phillips* Bible says,

> "Don't let the world around you squeeze you into its own mold, but let God remold your minds from within."

The subject of this verse is "you." *You* either allow the world to squeeze you or you forbid it. No one can mold you unless you allow it. You are the only one with authority over your thoughts. Notice what Jesus said in Matthew 18:18:

> "Believe me, whatever you forbid upon earth will be what is forbidden in Heaven, and whatever you permit on earth will

be what is permitted in Heaven" (*J.B. Phillips*).

You can change your future by making the decision to forbid wrong thoughts to continue to dominate your life. And when you make that decision, heaven will supply the power necessary to overcome those wrong thoughts.

The enemy will try to squeeze you into the world's mold with thoughts that declare: "You're a failure. You've always been a failure and you always will be. You will never amount to anything. You will never change so why bother."

Whose Report Will You Believe?

Has a doctor diagnosed you with an incurable disease in your body? Has someone told you that you aren't smart enough to attend college? Perhaps an employer concluded that you weren't qualified for a promotion? Or possibly you've heard a preacher say that Christians are nothing more than sinners saved by grace.

But whose report are you going to believe? Will you believe the doctor's diagnosis or God's prescription for healing? Isaiah 53:4-5 says:

"Surely He has borne our griefs and carried our sorrows; yet we esteemed Him stricken, smitten by God, and afflicted. But He was wounded for our transgressions, he was bruised for our iniquities; the chastisement for our peace was upon Him, and by His stripes we are healed" (*NKJ*).

Don't allow the negative attitude of others to plot the course for your destiny.

Instead, believe the report of the Lord.

Will you allow the opinion of others to stop you from getting the education you desire? Instead, believe what the Apostle Paul said: "We have the mind of Christ" (1 Corinthians 2:16). Agree with Solomon, the wisest man to live who said, "The memory of the righteous is blessed" (Proverbs 10:7).

Chapter 3

Strongholds of the Mind

If you have been weighed down with distorted thoughts a stronghold may have been built in your mind. Second Corinthians 10:4-5 says,

> "For the weapons of our warfare are not carnal but mighty in God for pulling down strongholds, casting down arguments and every high thing that exalts itself against the knowledge of God, bringing every thought into captivity to the obedience of Christ."

You may be wondering what a

stronghold is. The meaning of the Greek word is very interesting. Not only does it mean a fortress as you would suppose, but according to *Thayer's* definition it is an argument or reasoning used by one endeavoring to fortify his opinion and defend it against his opponent.

That's exactly what a stronghold of the mind does. It argues and reasons why God will not do what He has promised. A stronghold says, "It may work for others, but not for me."

God's Word is the only power that can overthrow and destroy every stronghold built in your mind.

Second Corinthians 10:4-5 assures you that God's weapons are mightier than any stronghold of the enemy. It doesn't matter what the stronghold is, or how long it's been there, God has promised that His weapons will destroy them!

How to Catch a Thief

You may be asking, "But *how* do I destroy the strongholds in my mind?" You destroy strongholds by simply following Paul's instructions to "take every thought captive."

The idea of taking a thought captive can be very elusive, but you capture a thought in the same way a thief is captured. In reality, wrong thoughts are thieves that come to steal God's promise of peace, health, joy, and prosperity.

Step #1: Identify the Thief

The first step you must take to capture a thief is to identify him. There is a simple, yet foolproof way to identify whether a thought is from God or not. Simply determine whether it brings abundant life or it steals, kills, or destroys. In John 10:10 Jesus said:

> "The thief comes only to steal, and kill, and destroy; I came that they might have life, and might have it abundantly."

If the thought in any way steals, kills, or destroys then you can be certain it is authored by your enemy, the devil. If it brings life, peace, and joy then it's from God. Philippians 4:8 instructs us to think on the things that are true, honest, right, pure, lovely, or worthy of praise.

Step #2: Arrest the Thief

When a thief is caught the arresting officer first reads his rights to him, then takes him into custody.

The moment you recognize a thought that steals the promise of God, arrest it and put a stop to it. Say right out loud, "Wrong thought, you have no right in my mind. My body is the temple of the Holy Spirit so you are trespassing on God's property. I command you to cease your actions against me and I render you powerless from this moment forward!"

Step #3: Pronounce Judgment

After a thief has been arrested he receives a judgment or a decree from a court of law.

Jesus has given the church legal power of attorney to use His name to enforce God's law. In John 14:13 Jesus said, "And whatever you ask in My name, that will I do, that the Father may be glorified in the Son."

Again, in Mark 16:17-18 Jesus left this commission to the church:

> "And these signs will accompany those who have believed: in My name they will cast out demons, they will speak with new tongues; they will pick up serpents, and if they drink any deadly poison, it shall not hurt them; they will lay hands on the sick, and they will recover."

Jesus has given the church—that's you and me—legal authority to use His name to cast out every demonic thought, argument, or reasoning that steals the inheritance God has promised—whether it relates to your finances, your family, your employment, or your health.

Boldly declare that the enemy no

longer has a right to your mind; that your days of distorted thinking are over. Job 22:28 says, "You will also decree a thing, and it will be established for you; and light will shine on your ways." When you speak it out loud you are making a decree in the spirit realm and it will be established.

That doesn't necessarily mean you will feel differently, or the circumstances will change immediately. But you must adopt the attitude that says, "If God said it, then that settles it!"

Step #4: Sentence the Thief

The final act of the court is to sentence a thief. That's what you must do with thoughts that steal God's promises. Sentence them to a rehabilitation program in God's Word that will transform them!

Ask the Holy Spirit to alert you the moment a wrong thought enters your mind, then put a stop to it. Jesus identified the Holy Spirit as your Helper. Why? Because His ministry is to help you whenever you need it! Most Christians don't take advantage of this wonderful, God-given gift of the Holy Spirit.

When the Helper alerts you to wrong thoughts, begin to rehabilitate them with the Word of God. The word *rehabilitate* means, "to restore, renovate, return to normalcy, refurbish, make whole again, reconstruct, rebuild and recondition." If you consistently follow this practice, it won't take very long before you gain control over the negative thoughts that have bombarded your mind for so long.

Conditioned to Fail

When a young elephant is added to

30

the circus, his trainer puts a heavy chain around his leg and drives a stake deep into the ground to prevent it from breaking loose and wandering away. The young, energetic elephant constantly tugs on the chain trying to break free, but eventually gives up.

When he becomes an adult, the trainer can tie him with a weak rope attached to a stake only a few inches long. He could easily break the bonds that confine him. But because he was "conditioned" as a young elephant, he now believes the thing on his leg that restrains him is more powerful than he is.

Many Christians have become conditioned to believe that they are unable to break free from their distorted thinking. These misguided thoughts must literally undergo a renovation, much like a building would—tearing down the old thought process and replacing it with new thoughts. In Ephesians 4:22-24 Paul commands us to do just that:

> "Lay aside the old self, which is being corrupted in accordance with the lusts of deceit, and that you be renewed in the spirit of your mind, and put on the new self, which in the likeness of God has been created in righteousness and holiness of the truth."

Like with any renovation process, it takes time, but it's not impossible! And the rewards will far exceed the effort.

Resetting the Direction of Life

God has supplied you with the comprehensive equipment you need to complete this renovation process. Second

Timothy 3:16 says from the *Phillips* translation:

> "All scripture is inspired by God and is useful for teaching the faith and correcting error, for resetting the direction of a man's life and training him in good living. The scriptures are the comprehensive equipment of the man of God, and fit him fully for all branches of his work."

God's Word is able to reset the course of your life regardless of the nature of your distorted thoughts—whether they relate to your health, your finances, your employment, or your relationships.

Search the Bible for Scriptures that specifically address your problem and write them down on a 3 X 5 card. Each time your thoughts drift off course, pull out the card and begin replacing the distorted thoughts with God's Word.

In the evening, before you drift off to sleep, go over the verses in your mind. Don't allow yourself to go to sleep until you can remember at least one. You may have to get out of bed to read them again, but eventually with enough practice they will flow from your heart with ease. This is more than a memorization program— it's the living Word of God remolding you from within.

Then in the morning, before you get out of bed remember those Scriptures again. If you practice this regularly they will become rooted and established in your heart and that's when your life will begin to change dramatically!

Chapter 4

Transforming A Distorted Image

Y ou can change distorted images by simply looking into an accurate mirror that reflects the true you. James 1:23-25 says,

> "For if anyone is a hearer of the word and not a doer, he is like a man who looks at his natural face in a mirror; for once he has looked at himself and gone away, he has immediately forgotten what kind of person he was.
>
> "But one who looks intently at the perfect law, the law of liberty,

and abides by it, not having become a forgetful hearer but an effectual doer, this man shall be blessed in what he does."

If changing a distorted image only required hearing the Word of God preached, then everyone in church would be transformed. Instead, James gives three important ingredients that contribute to change. He said you must look intently, abide in the Word, and be a doer of the Word.

And he cautions those who take a casual attitude toward God's Word. It is this man who is destined to forget what he has seen and as a result, fail to receive the promise of God.

The solution for this inattentive attitude is first to look intently—that means persistently and purposefully—into God's Word. Second, James admonishes you to abide or remain in the Word until it permeates your being. And finally, you must act on the Word. Without corresponding actions your convictions and good intentions are of little value.

The Word of God Is A Mirror

The Apostle Paul also used the illustration of a mirror in transforming our distorted thoughts. We read in 2 Corinthians 3:18:

> "And all of us, as with unveiled face, because we continued to behold in the Word of God as a mirror the glory of the Lord, are constantly being transfigured into His very own image in ever increasing splendor and from one degree of glory to another" (*AMP*).

God's Word does just what your mir-

ror does when you look into it each morning—it reflects your image. And if you
look anything like I do when I get up in
the morning, you have your work cut
out for you!

When I look into the mirror, I see the
many things that need change and that
motivates me into action! I fix my hair,
put on make up, change my clothes and
do whatever is required until the image in
the mirror is transformed.

The worst thing I could do would be
to look into the mirror and decide it is
hopeless and walk away unchanged.

Paul wrote that God's Word
functions like a mirror—it reveals the
things that need to be changed. We make
a grave mistake when we casually look
into the mirror of God's Word and walk

away before being transformed. We must abide in the Word and do whatever is required until the image in the mirror is transformed into God's very own image.

But be forewarned: One look will not bring about a transformation! Instead, as you continue to look into the mirror, little by little you will be transfigured from glory to glory.

Chapter 5

Meditation is the Key

T he key to transforming distorted thoughts is meditating on the Word of God. Meditation is a simple yet powerful practice. Instead of allowing whatever pops into your mind control your thought process, make the decision to purposely meditate on the Word of God.

When God appointed Joshua to lead Israel into the promised land, He gave him these critical instructions:

"This book of the law shall not depart from your mouth, but you shall meditate on it day and night, so that you may be careful to do according to all that is written in it; for then you will make your way prosperous, and then you will have success" (Joshua 1:8).

Meditation is not simply reading your Bible day and night—no one, not even ministers are able to do that. Meditation holds three important meanings to the believer.

Muse or Ponder the Word

The first definition of *meditate* is "to muse." *Muse* actually means to "ponder, consider and study closely." The following verses express the importance of meditating by musing or pondering.

"I will meditate on all Thy work, and muse on Thy deeds" (Psalm 77:12).

"I remember the days of old; I meditate on all Thy doings; I muse on the work of Thy hands" (Psalm 143:5).

Psalm 77:6 says, "I will remember my song in the night; I will meditate with my heart; and my spirit ponders."

Chewing the Cud

The second definition of *meditation* and probably the most vivid illustration is that of a cow chewing her cud. First, the cow takes a mouthful of grass, chews it, then swallows it. Later, she regurgitates that same mouthful of grass and chews it once more only to swallow it again.

This process of chewing, swallowing, and regurgitating to chew it again is repeated over and over until the grass is so refined that it becomes a part of her being.

Meditating on the Word of God accomplishes in your heart exactly what the cow accomplishes when she chews her cud.

When an adverse situation that doesn't line up with God's Word threatens you—sickness, lack, depression, or strife—find Scriptures that address the issue and begin chewing on them, pondering them over and over. Then when you must attend to other business, swallow it and bring it up when you are free to chew on it again.

The more you meditate on the Scripture the more refined it becomes until eventually it becomes a part of your being, like the grass the cow chews. Meditating on the Word of God in this manner will greatly influence your mind, will, and emotions.

Muttering God's Word

Meditation also includes muttering the Word. Not only are you to ponder and chew on the Word but you are to continually speak it out of your mouth. In this manner meditation occupies both your conversation and your confession.

Everyone knows how to mutter. Muttering is to speak things quietly or under your breath, speaking to yourself regardless of whether people are present to hear you. You may mutter while driving your car or washing the dishes.

Have you ever misplaced something and asked yourself, "Where did I put that? Where is the last place I remember seeing it?" That is muttering. It's easy to understand how meditating by muttering can be done any time or any place.

When important decisions need to be made, you can mutter to yourself something similar to this: "Jesus has made wisdom available to me. I have the mind of Christ. In Christ are hidden all the treasures of wisdom and knowledge and He dwells in me. The Holy Spirit, Who is my Helper, will reveal the answer to me."

By doing this you put yourself in position to make your way prosperous and be successful.

Put A Stop to Worry

Meditation on the Word of God will bring your mind and emotions under control. It is the most powerful tool to stop worry and become master over your thoughts.

"Let the words of my mouth and

the meditation of my heart be acceptable in Thy sight, O Lord, my rock and my Redeemer" (Psalm 19:14).

Make a determination to embrace what the Word of God says by imagining yourself living in the plan and will of God—regardless of your present circumstances.

Speaking Aloud

The Hebrew word in Joshua 1:8 translated *meditate* is rendered "to speak" in the following verses:

"For my mouth will speak truth; wickedness is an abomination to my lips" (Proverbs 8:7, *NKJV*).

"And my tongue shall speak of thy

righteousness and of thy praise all the day long" (Psalm 35:28, *KJV*).

"The mouth of the righteous speaketh wisdom, and his tongue talketh of judgment" (Psalm 37:30, *KJV*).

God instructs us, like He did the children of Israel, to speak about His mighty deeds accomplished throughout our lives. Ephesians 5:19 expresses it this way:

"Speaking to one another in psalms and hymns and spiritual songs, singing and making melody with your heart to the Lord."

Speaking aloud serves a dual purpose—it benefits both the one telling of the wondrous deeds of God and the one hearing them. Psalms 78:6-7 says,

"That the generation to come might know, even the children yet to be born, that they may arise and tell them to their children, that they should put their confidence in God, and not forget the works of God, but keep His commandments" (*NKJV*).

When you tell others about the works God has performed on your behalf you are encouraging and edifying yourself. First, it builds your confidence—not in yourself, but in God Who has delivered you from danger.

According to Revelation 12:11 your own testimony will cause you to become an overcomer: "And they overcame him because of the blood of the Lamb and because of the word of their testimony."

The second benefit of speaking the

Word aloud is to testify to the one hearing of the miracle working power of God. You become what the Apostle Paul described as a letter known and read by all men (2 Corinthians 3:2). You become a witness before their eyes of someone who has been a recipient of God's love. And if He will do it for you, He will do it for others as well.

Chapter 6

Proof of Love

W hat you love is evidenced by what you think about. Psalm 119:97 says, "O how I love Thy law! It is my meditation all the day."

David loved the Word of God. That's why it was his meditation day and night. It wasn't that he had nothing better to do. After all, He was the King of Israel and his day was occupied with the business of the kingdom.

David not only read the book of the law, but he incorporated what he read into his thoughts. Notice the benefit of meditation: "I have more understanding than all my teachers, for Your testimonies are my meditation" (Psalms 119:99).

When you begin to meditate the Word of God, you will have illumination and understanding of how to walk in what God is revealing to you.

Self-Imposed Discipline

In order to master your thoughts, you must make demands on yourself. You have to become your own taskmaster. You become more demanding on yourself than anyone would dare. No one could push you as hard as you push yourself.

In 1 Corinthians 9:24-25 the Apostle Paul compares the discipline of the Christian life to that of an athlete:

"Do you not know that those

who run in a race all run, but only one receives the prize? Run in such a way that you may win. And everyone who competes in the games exercises self-control in all things. They then do it to receive a perishable wreath, but we an imperishable."

Athletes who want to win a race don't require discipline to be imposed upon them; they enforce their own discipline. Others may indulge in a variety of pleasures, but the runner disciplines and restrains himself.

Notice Paul said those who compete, exercise self-control "in all things." Not only does he eat a very controlled diet, but he also denies himself of many commonplace activities to prepare for the race. Regrettably the athlete often exceeds the self-imposed discipline of most Christians.

Pastor Ezell, the man who trained us in ministry, was the most disciplined man I have ever known. The godly principles that governed his life marked my life so deeply that I have adopted most as my own. I was a young believer during this time of training and I was often confused by the undisciplined and self-indulgent lifestyle of some Christians. But he would set me back on track by calmly reciting an adage that he lived by: "Others may, but I may not." This self-imposed discipline taught me the importance of personal restraint.

If we expect to win the prize at the end of the race of life then we must keep our focus on the Word of God. It's not our job to judge whether others apply the

Word. That's the job of the Holy Spirit. It's a full time job keeping up with what God has called us to do as individuals.

Practice the Word of God

The Bible makes it clear that we are to put God's Word into practice in order to train our five physical senses. Without training our sense to obey the Word of God we will continue to live a life dominated by the flesh.

"But solid food is for the mature, who because of practice have their senses trained to discern good and evil" (Hebrews 5:14).

This scripture reveals that it is by practice or exercise that our five physical senses are trained to obey the Word of God. If we fail to discipline our senses they will dictate and dominate our lives. Peter also emphasizes the importance of practicing what the Word teaches us.

> "Therefore, brethren, be all the more diligent to make certain about His calling and choosing you; for as long as you practice these things, you will never stumble" (2 Peter 1:10).

What an amazing statement! If we are diligent to put the Word into practice we can be assured that we will never stumble or fall.

Paul said that when we practice what the Word teaches us, the peace of God will be with us.

> "Finally, brethren, whatever is true, whatever is honorable,

whatever is right, whatever is pure, whatever is lovely, whatever is of good repute, if there is any excellence and if anything worthy of praise, let your mind dwell on these things. The things you have learned and received and heard and seen in me, practice these things; and the God of peace shall be with you" (Philippians 4:8-9).

We are instructed to not only dwell on these things but practice them fervently. In other words, take inventory of your thought life. If you are dwelling on and practicing anything other then these things you cannot expect the peace of God to rule in your heart.

Peace is a commodity sought after by people in every class of society. But God has promised it to those who would center their thoughts on Him. Isaiah 26:3 promises, "He will keep in perfect peace all those who trust in him, whose thoughts turn often to the Lord!" (*The Living Bible*).

Search Me, O God

David was a man of integrity in his walk with God. He asked the Lord to not only examine his heart but also test his thoughts. If God found anything that caused Him sorrow or grief, David invited God to change his course.

> "Search me, O God, and know my heart; try me and know my anxious thoughts; and see if there be any hurtful way in me, and lead me in the everlasting way" (Psalm 139:23-24).

Ask the Lord to search your heart

and identify the distorted thoughts that have stolen your rightful inheritance. Then co-operate with the Holy Spirit to rehabilitate them and begin the transformation process today!

Start your day, armed with *the* Truth.

So many will begin their mornings tuning in to TV news, or fill the quiet with the empty banter of early morning secular talk shows. We all know starting off right can prepare us for victory. Why not fuel up with strength-boosting encouragement and insights from God's Word?

Following are just a few testimonies from the growing number of believers who have chosen to brighten their mornings with the light of God's Word through the DBM *Enriching Life Daily* devotional emails:

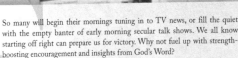

"Thank you for saying yes to the Lord and following after His heart. Your daily inspirationals are so anointed... clear, precise and Life giving. You and Dennis follow the heart beat of the Lord. Jesus continue to bless all you put your hand to and increase your circle of influence for His Kingdom. Much love in Him..."

"Thank you for this email, it was exactly what I needed today. God bless you for the work you are doing in extending God's kingdom."

"Thank you for your daily emails...they are such a blessing to me and help me with my walk with God. I look forward to them everyday and they encourage me in God's Word daily! I am so thankful for God bringing you into my life through my church. You are awesome and thank you so so much! Blessing to you both..."

testimonies

Try *Enriching Life Daily* with Vikki Burke!
DennisBurkeMinistries.org

Other
practical
resources from
Vikki Burke

Aim Your Child Like an Arrow

"For those of you with the responsibility of raising a family, I know this book will be an invaluable tool that you will refer to many times as you seek to apply God's truths to training your children or grandchildren. Vikki is a great communicator of these truths, and her 'how to' applications are practical and insightful. In today's society with so many dysfunctional families, it is refreshing to know that the Word of God is still the answer.

Vikki Burke is a mother who has applied God's Word in raising her child. Her daughter Jessica is a young woman who reflects her parents' dedication to biblical training. She is a credit to the values they have instilled in her. As a mother and grandmother, I take the responsibility of continuing to instill the Word of God into my children and grandchildren very seriously. In reading this book, I was blessed and found fresh inspiration for ministering to my family. You will too."

—Carolyn Savelle

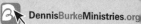